My First Book of Hymns and Spirituals

26 Favorite Songs in Easy Piano Arrangements

Bergerac

With Illustrations by
Thea Kliros

DOVER PUBLICATIONS, INC.
Mineola, New York

à Nicole

Making up a song, or singing a song that you heard somewhere, is a way to share feelings—to let someone know that you're happy or sad, or just to tell the world how you feel about things in your life. The tunes and words in our book are just like that, but most are very old and very special because they fly us *backwards*—like a magical musical carpet—to what it was like to live almost 200 years ago! . . . to everyday life on the farms, on the plantations, and in the towns and churches of 19th-century America.

Hymns and spirituals are songs of prayer and praise to the Lord. Some share the joy of the harvest and a life of plenty, while others dream of a journey from a life of bondage and sadness to a life of freedom and peace. Some songs are quiet prayers, told in plain, every-day words. Others are happy outbursts of *Hallelujahs!* and pieces of Holy Scripture. There are plantation melodies and slave songs from the Deep South, and rugged old church tunes sung by descendants of America's colonial founders.

All of young America is here, telling us what they thought, what they felt, and how they prayed.

Copyright

Copyright © 1999 by Dover Publications, Inc.
All rights reserved under Pan American and International Copyright Conventions.

Bibliographical Note

My First Book of Hymns and Spirituals: 26 Favorite Songs in Easy Piano Arrangements
is a new work, first published by Dover Publications, Inc., in 1999.

International Standard Book Number: 0-486-40849-3

Manufactured in the United States of America
Dover Publications, Inc., 31 East 2nd Street, Mineola, N.Y. 11501

Contents

The Gift to Be Simple

Simply, but not too slow

Traditional song of the Shakers, a religious
community of 19th-century America

This Train

Imagining a train carrying slaves
to a place of freedom and peace

The train chugs and chugs as it
slowly gets up steam. . .

(. . . going faster. . .   and faster. . .   and faster. . .   until. . .)

Roaring right along, full of joy!

"This train   is   bound for glo - ry,   this train,___

"This train   is   bound for glo - ry,   this train,___

6

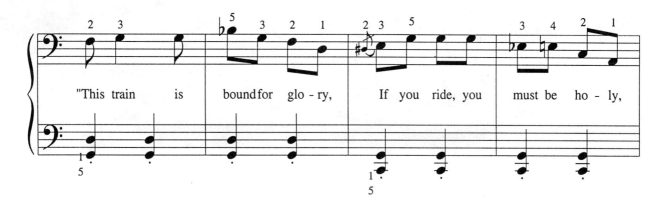

"This train is boundfor glo - ry, If you ride, you must be ho - ly,

(Hear that whistle goin' 'round the bend)

"This train..."

(Slowly disappearing down the track)

(hold the chord!)

(slower and slower. . .   quieter and quieter. . .)

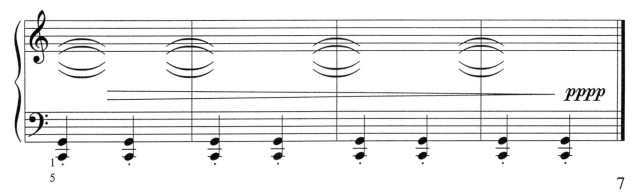

pppp

Go, Tell It on the Mountain

Telling a story (not too fast)

A song glorifying the birth
of the Holy Infant Jesus

While shep – herds kept their watch – ing O'er

si – lent flocks by night, Be – hold through – out the

heav – ens there shone a ho – ly light, _____

Bright and lively

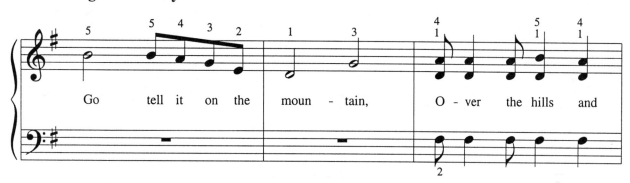

Go tell it on the moun - tain, O - ver the hills and

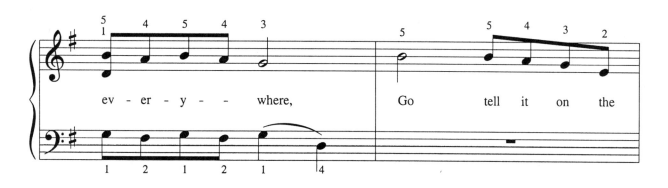

ev - er - y - - where, Go tell it on the

moun - tain that Je - sus Christ___ is born!

9

Deep River

Seeking "the promised land" across the mythical river Jordan—a safe-haven of peace, love and plenty

In a quiet mood

10

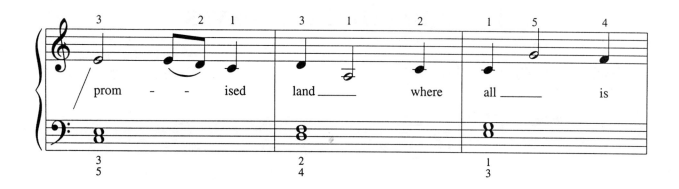

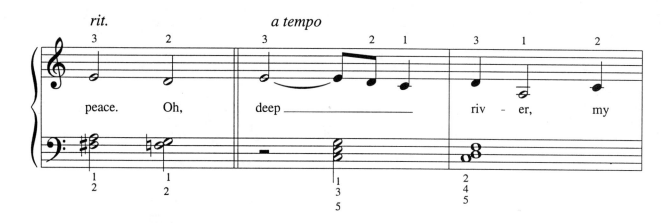

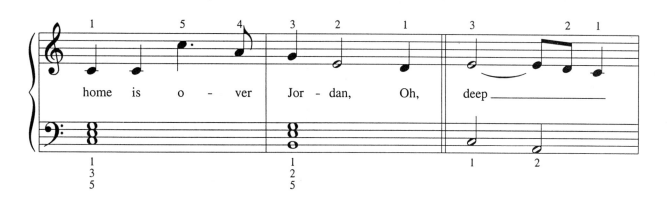

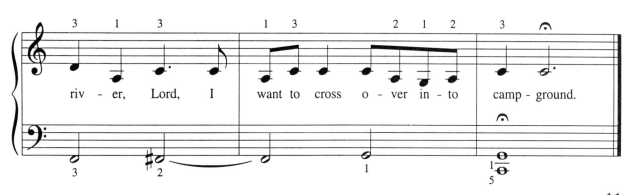

Bringing in the Sheaves

Words by Knowles Shaw
Music by George A. Minor

Bright and lively (but not too fast)

Swing Low, Sweet Chariot

Moving along, with a gentle swing

Dreaming of a sweet journey to a heavenly rest far from slavery

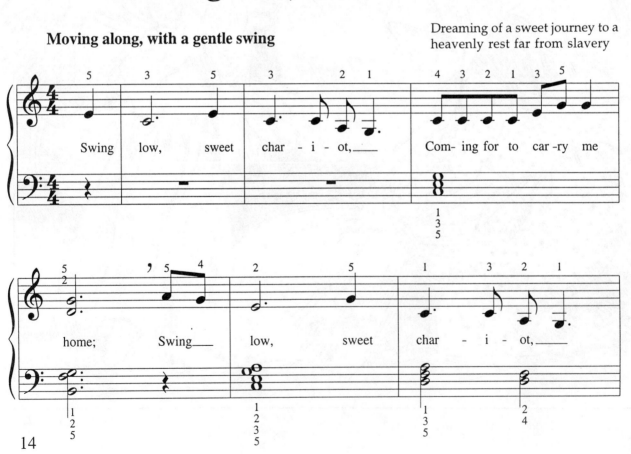

14

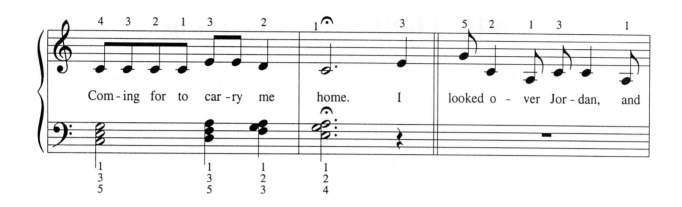

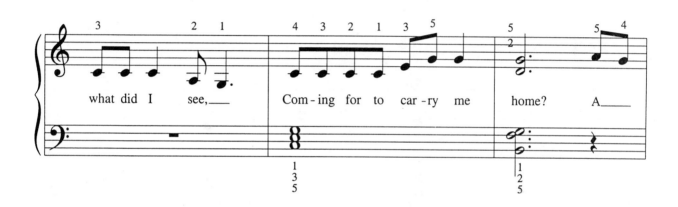

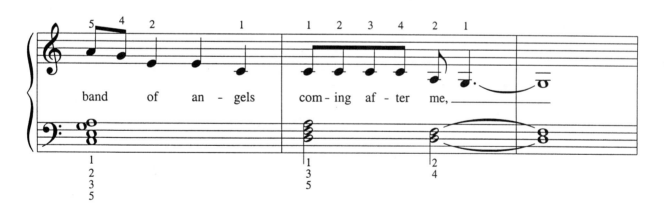

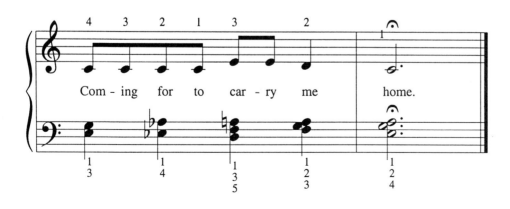

15

Come, Thou Almighty King

Words by Charles Wesley
Music by Felice Giardini

With a stately, even pace

16

God of Our Fathers

With solemn majesty

Words by George W. Warren
Music by Daniel C. Roberts

God of our fa - thers, whose al - might - y hand

Leads forth in beau - ty all the star - ry band;

Of shin - ing worlds in splen - dor through the skies,

Our grate - ful songs be - fore Thy throne a - rise.

Gimme That Ol'- Time Religion

Full of life and bounce!

A joyful spiritual, calling one
and all to rejoice in the Good Lord

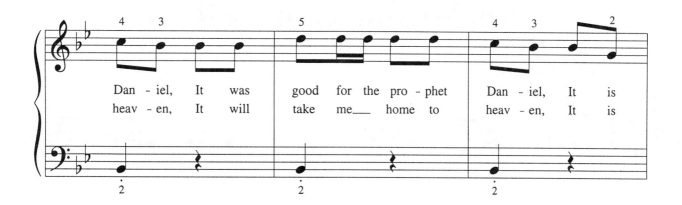

Dan - iel, It was / heav - en, It will

good for the pro - phet / take me___ home to

Dan - iel, It is / heav - en, It is

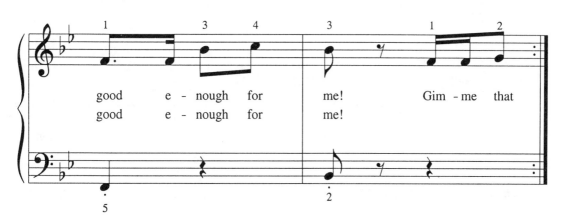

good e - nough for / good e - nough for

me! / me!

Gim - me that

Shall We Gather at the River?

Words and music
by Rev. Robert Lowry

At a moderate pace

Onward, Christian Soldiers

Words by Rev. Sabine Baring-Gould
Music by Arthur S. Sullivan

Sturdy and steady!

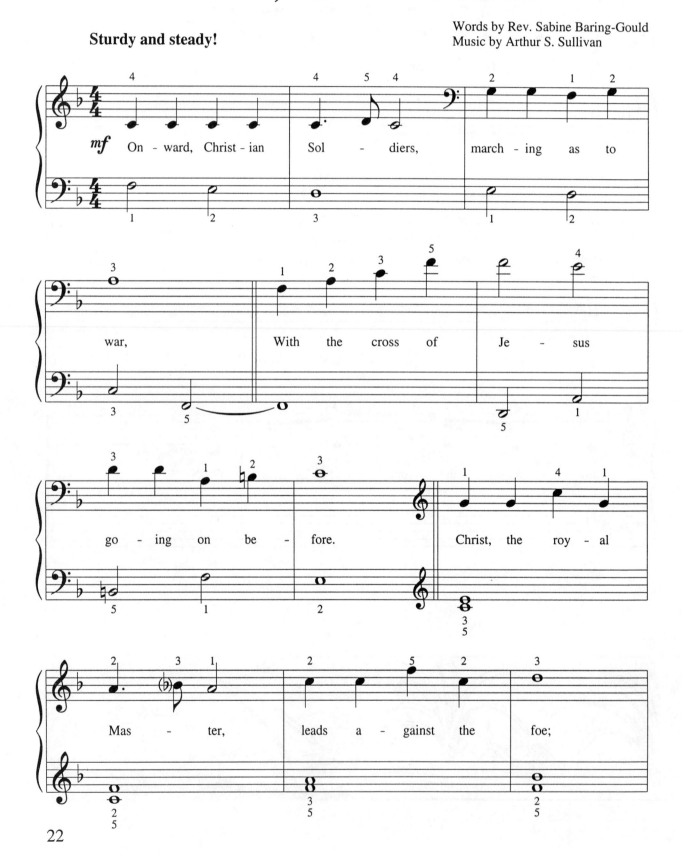

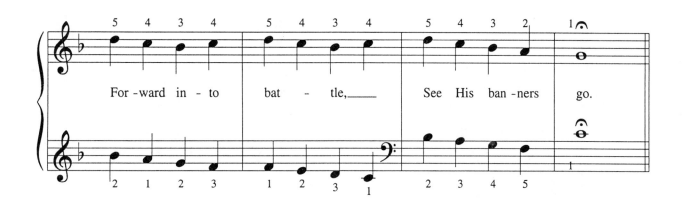

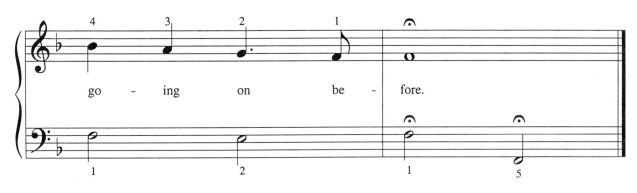

He's Got the Whole World
in His Hand

Simply, with a slightly jazzy beat

One of the most joyous and popular
spirituals ever sung (with many verses!)

25

Praise God
from Whom All Blessings Flow
("Old Hundred")

The words of Psalm 134, set to music
by Louis Bourgeois in the 16th century

Flowing

Holy! Holy! Holy!
Lord God Almighty!

Words by Reginald Heber
Music by John B. Dykes

Broad, steady, strong

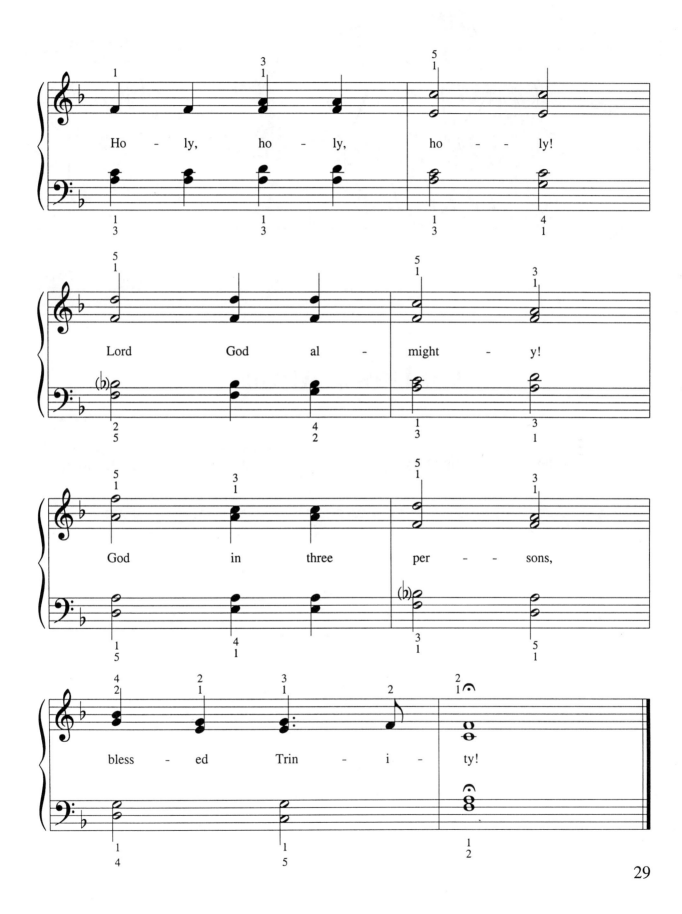

Go Down, Moses

Slowly, telling a very old story

The world's most famous song about the pains of slavery and the hunger for freedom

When Is - rael was in E - gypt's land

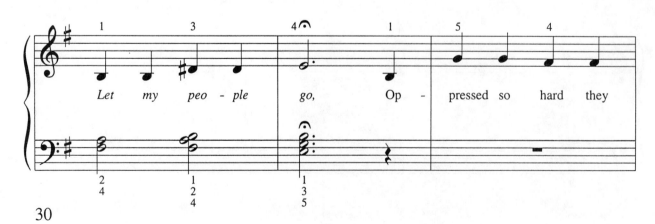

Let my peo - ple go, Op - pressed so hard they

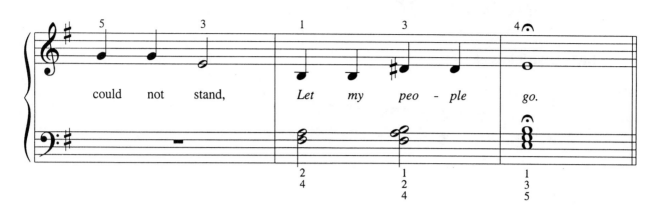

could not stand,   *Let   my   peo - ple*   *go.*

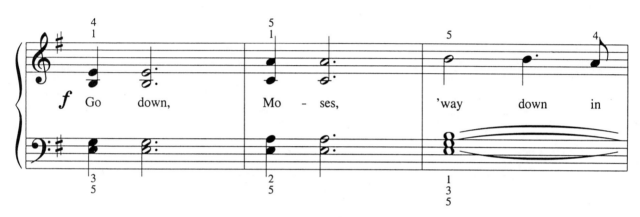

f Go   down,   Mo - ses,   'way   down   in

gradually softer and slower

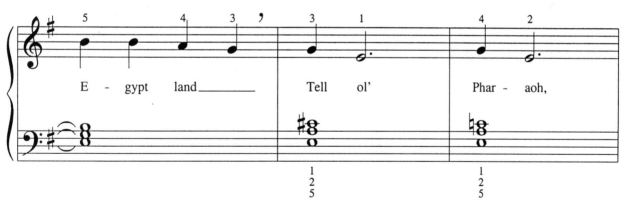

E - gypt land_____   Tell   ol'   Phar - aoh,

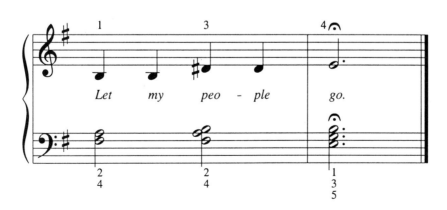

Let   my   peo - ple   go.

Joshua Fought the Battle of Jericho

Lively, with lots of zest!

A famous Bible story, set to music

Slow *(play it three times)*

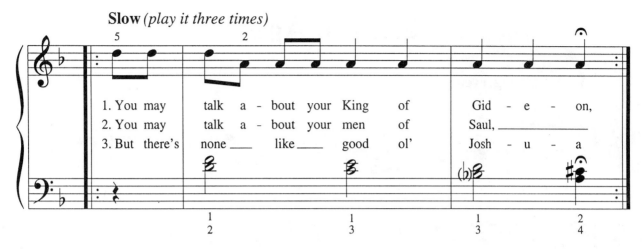

1. You may talk a - bout your King of Gid - e - on,
2. You may talk a - bout your men of Saul, _____
3. But there's none ___ like ___ good ol' Josh - u - a

Fast again

At the bat - tle of Jer - i - cho!

Go back to the beginning, then stop at "End here"

Rock of Ages

With a strong, even pace

Words by Augustus M. Toplady (1776)
Music by Thomas Hastings (1832)

Rock of a - ges, cleft for me, Let me hide my - self in

Thee; Let the wa - ter and the blood From Thy

wound - ed side which flowed Be of sin the dou - ble

cure, Save from wrath and make me pure.

Nearer, My God, to Thee

Gently, but moving along

Words by Sarah F. Adams
Music by Lowell Mason

Kumbayah

A sweet, gentle prayer

African folk song

Some - one's   sing - ing, Lord,   Kum - ba - yah,

Some - one's   weep - ing, Lord,   Kum - ba - yah,

36

We Gather Together

(Thanksgiving Prayer)

An anonymous song of thanks
based on a 17th-century Dutch hymn

A quiet prayer, gently flowing

Were You There?

A lament, slow and sustained

A spiritual about shared sorrows

40

Amazing Grace

Slowly flowing

Probably America's greatest folk hymn, sung by people everywhere

A Mighty Fortress Is Our God

Original German words by Martin Luther
English words by Frederick H. Hedge
Melody based on plainchant

Broad, strong

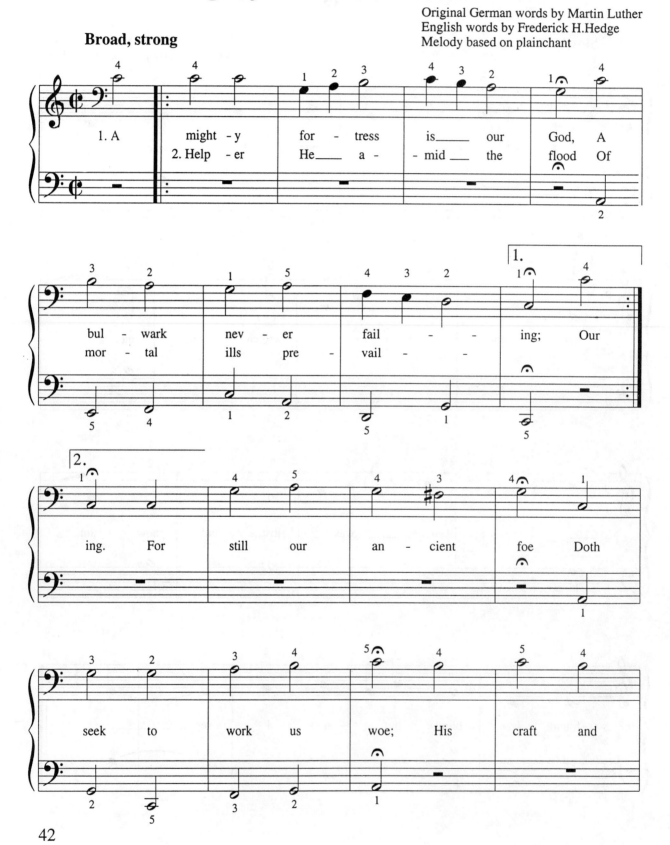

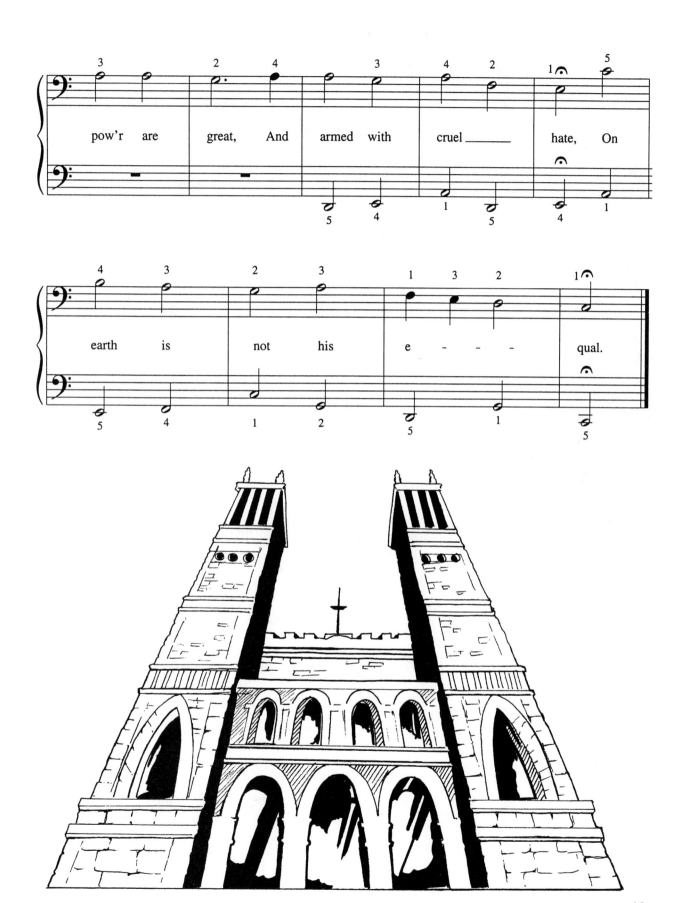

pow'r are great, And armed with cruel _____ hate, On

earth is not his e - - - qual.

Sometimes I Feel
Like a Motherless Child

A lament for a lost,
far-away homeland

Gently, but not too slow

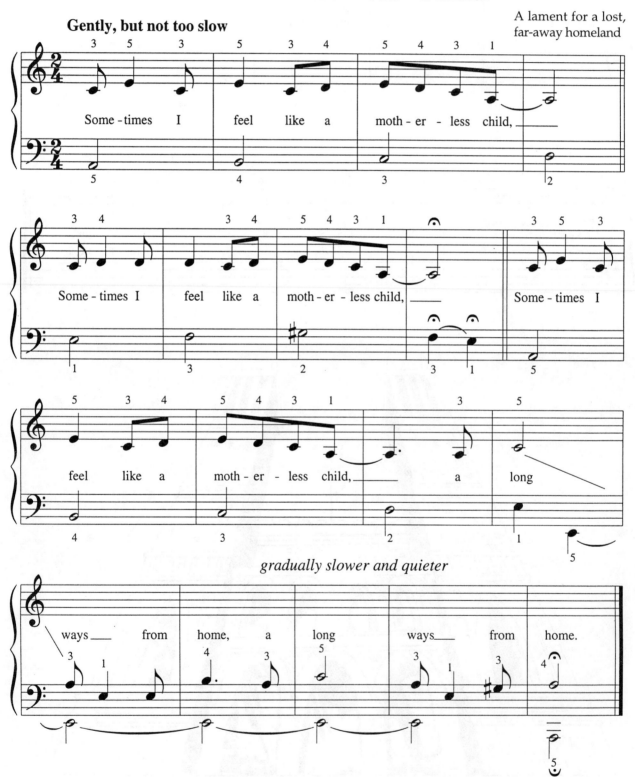

gradually slower and quieter

Nobody Knows the Trouble I've Seen

Very slow, very quiet

A spiritual well-known about the
time of America's Civil War (1865)

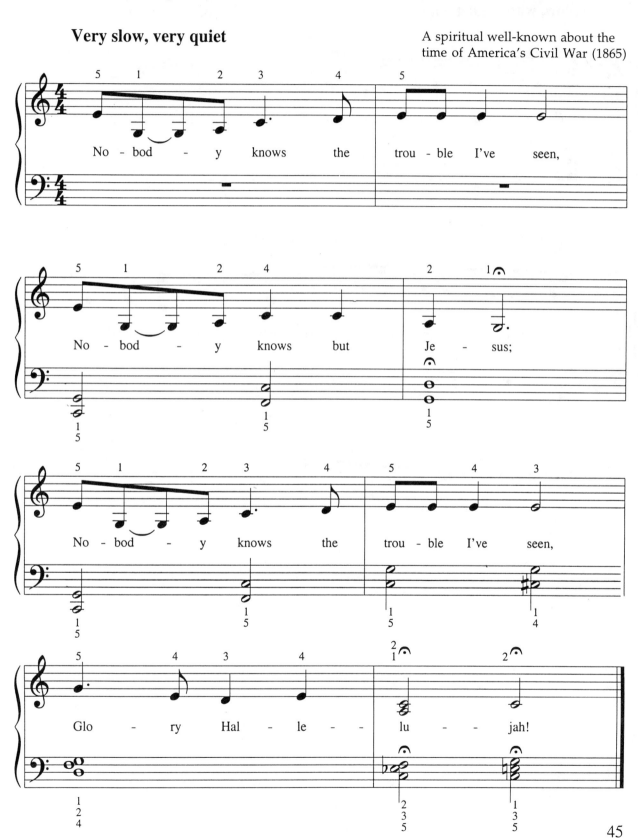

Glory! Hallelujah!
(Battle Hymn of the Republic)

Words by Julia Ward Howe
Music: "Glory, Hallelujah" (Anon.)

Slow, with a quiet majesty

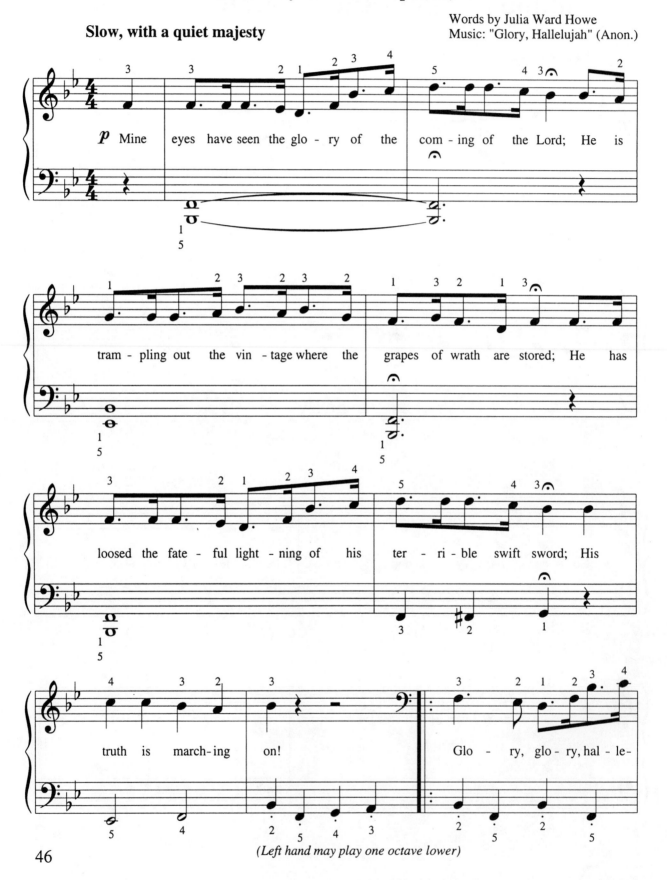

Mine eyes have seen the glo - ry of the com - ing of the Lord; He is

tram - pling out the vin - tage where the grapes of wrath are stored; He has

loosed the fate - ful light - ning of his ter - ri - ble swift sword; His

truth is march - ing on! Glo - ry, glo - ry, hal - le -

(Left hand may play one octave lower)

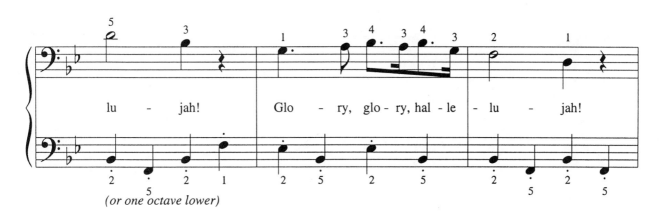

lu - jah! Glo - ry, glo - ry, hal - le - lu - jah!

(or one octave lower)

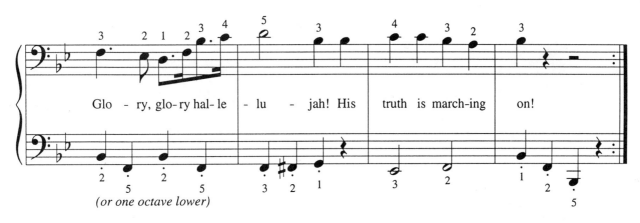

Glo - ry, glo-ry hal- le - lu - jah! His truth is march-ing on!

(or one octave lower)